A LIFEBUILDER

SUFFERING

Receiving God's Comfort

*10 Studies
for individuals or groups*

Jack Kuhatschek

With Notes for Leaders

SCRIPTURE UNION
130 City Road, London EC1V 2NJ

© 1992 by Jack Kuhatschek

First published in the United States by InterVarsity Press.
First published in Great Britain by Scripture Union, 1993.

Cover photograph: Robert McKendrick

ISBN 0 86201 851 X

Printed in England by Ebenezer Baylis & Son Limited, The Trinity Press, Worcester and London

Contents

Getting the Most from LifeBuilder Bible Studies — 5

Introducing Suffering — 8

1 **When Your World Falls Apart**   Job 1—2   *10*

2 **Praying Our Pain**   Psalm 6   *14*

3 **Waiting for the Lord**   Psalm 27   *18*

4 **The God of All Comfort**   2 Corinthians 1:3-11   *21*

5 **The Power of Weakness**   2 Corinthians 12:1-10   *24*

6 **Wounds That Heal**   Hebrews 12:1-13   *28*

7 **Suffering for Christ**   Acts 5:12-42   *32*

8 **The Suffering God**   Mark 15:1-39   *36*

9 **The Death of Death**   1 Corinthians 15   *40*

10 **The Shattered Silence**   Job 38:1-41; 40:1-14; 42:1-6   *44*

Leader's Notes — 47

Getting the Most
from LifeBuilder Bible Studies

Many of us long to fill our minds and our lives with Scripture. We desire to be transformed by its message. LifeBuilder Bible Studies are designed to be an exciting and challenging way to do just that. They help us to be guided by God's Word in every area of life.

How They Work

LifeBuilders have a number of distinctive features. Perhaps the most important is that they are *inductive* rather than *deductive*. In other words, they lead us to *discover* what the Bible says rather than simply *telling* us what it says.

They are also thought-provoking. They help us to think about the meaning of the passage so that we can truly understand what the author is saying. The questions require more than one-word answers.

The studies are personal. Questions expose us to the promises, assurances, exhortations and challenges of God's Word. They are designed to allow the Scriptures to renew our minds so that we can be transformed by the Spirit of God. This is the ultimate goal of all Bible study.

The studies are versatile. They are designed for student, neighborhood and church groups. They are also effective for individual study.

How They're Put Together

LifeBuilders also have a distinctive format. Each study need take no more than forty-five minutes in a group setting or thirty minutes in personal study – unless you choose to take more time.

The studies can be used within a quarter system in a church and fit well in a semester or trimester system on a college campus. If a guide has more than thirteen studies, it is divided into two or occasionally three parts of approximately twelve studies each.

LifeBuilders use a workbook format. Space is provided for writing answers to each question. This is ideal for personal study and allows group members to prepare in advance for the discussion.

The studies also contain leader's notes. They show how to lead a group discussion, provide additional background information on certain questions, give helpful tips on group dynamics and suggest ways to deal with problems which may arise during the discussion. With such helps, someone with little or no experience can lead an effective study.

Suggestions for Individual Study

1. As you begin each study, pray that God will help you to understand and apply the passage to your life.

2. Read and reread the assigned Bible passage to familiarize yourself with what the author is saying. In the case of book studies, you may want to read through the entire book prior to the first study. This will give you a helpful overview of its contents.

3. A good modern translation of the Bible, rather than the King James Version or a paraphrase, will give you the most help. The New International Version, the New American Standard Bible and the Revised Standard Version are all recommended. However, the questions in this guide are based on the New International Version.

4. Write your answers in the space provided in the study guide. This will help you to express your understanding of the passage clearly.

5. It might be good to have a Bible dictionary handy. Use it to look up any unfamiliar words, names or places.

Suggestions for Group Study

1. Come to the study prepared. Follow the suggestions for individual study mentioned above. You will find that careful preparation will greatly enrich your time spent in group discussion.

2. Be willing to participate in the discussion. The leader of your group will not be lecturing. Instead, he or she will be encouraging the members of the group to discuss what they have learned from the passage. The leader will be asking the questions that are found in this guide. Plan to share what God has taught you in your individual study.

3. Stick to the passage being studied. Your answers should be based on the verses which are the focus of the discussion and not on outside authorities such as commentaries or speakers. This guide deliberately avoids jumping from book to book or passage to passage. Each study focuses on only one passage. Book studies are generally designed to lead you through the book in the order in which it was written. This will help you follow the author's argument.

4. Be sensitive to the other members of the group. Listen attentively when they share what they have learned. You may be surprised by their insights! Link what you say to the comments of others so the group stays on the topic. Also, be affirming whenever you can. This will encourage some of the more hesitant members of the group to participate.

5. Be careful not to dominate the discussion. We are sometimes so eager to share what we have learned that we leave too little opportunity for others to respond. By all means participate! But allow others to also.

6. Expect God to teach you through the passage being discussed and through the other members of the group. Pray that you will have an enjoyable and profitable time together.

7. If you are the discussion leader, you will find additional suggestions and helpful ideas for each study in the leader's notes. These are found at the back of the guide.

Introducing Suffering

In the book *All Quiet on the Western Front* the author, Erich Remarque, describes the horrors of front-line battle in World War 1. In the preface he writes:

> This book is to be neither an accusation nor a confession, and least of all an adventure, for death is not an adventure to those who stand face to face with it. It will try simply to tell of a generation of men who, even though they may have escaped its shells, were destroyed by the War.

Suffering has enormous power. For some that power is destructive—it tears their hearts, wounds their spirits, and leaves them broken and scarred for life. Suffering can turn healthy people into cynical, bitter distortions of their former selves.

Yet what a mystery! Suffering also has the positive power to transform us. My grandmother is an excellent example. Her firstborn son died of a staph infection when he was twenty. Her third child was born a dwarf. Her husband became an alcoholic and died when he was sixty-five (she outlived him by twenty years). And yet she emerged with a beauty and inner grace that could only have been forged in the intense heat of suffering.

My own experience with suffering has been somewhere in between. There is a time I refer to as "my former life"—a period of years when I felt overwhelmed with anguish in my relationships and ministry. Although nearly a decade has passed since that time, like Jacob I walk with an emotional limp that may never go away (see Gen 32). But just as Jacob hobbled off with God's blessing, so my weakness opened me up to God's grace, and my helplessness led me to trust in his tender care.

The fact that suffering's effects are so varied should warn us against analyzing suffering itself. Instead, we should focus our attention on the *people* who suffer and why they respond to it well or poorly.

That is what these Bible studies will attempt to do. We will sit with Job in the ashes as he cries out for answers from the Lord. We will listen to Paul's prayer as he begs God to pull out a painful thorn. We will discover why David's fear is replaced by strength and confidence when he is surrounded by enemies. And we will consider the supreme example of suffering and triumph—the Lord himself.

We can never escape from suffering in a fallen world. Neither can we mystically rise above the wounds it inflicts. But we *can* learn to endure it in a way that brings personal growth and glory to God.

1
When Your World Falls Apart

Job 1–2

On the morning of April 18, 1906, the San Andreas fault settled violently, and San Francisco was shaken by a terrible earthquake. Huge cracks opened up in the earth, buildings shuddered and collapsed, and fire swept through the city, leaving it virtually destroyed. Thousands who went to bed peacefully the night before awoke to a world that had fallen apart around them.

If seismic devices could measure personal tragedy, then Job's "earthquake" would have registered 8.5 on the Richter scale. In one day he lost everything he owned and almost everyone he held dear. Because of what Job endured and the way he endured it, his name has become synonymous with suffering.

Yet even though Job's suffering was extreme, it was by no means unique. In one form or another, his story is re-enacted every day in a broken and fallen world. During such times, we find that Job personifies our grief and our painful sense of loss.

---

1. Think of a time in your life when your world seemed to fall apart. What were some of the thoughts and feelings you experienced?

2. Read Job 1. In Greek tragedy the greatness of the main character emphasizes the heights from which he falls. In a similar way, how do verses 1-5 set the stage for the tragedy that follows?

3. At the outset of the story, why do you think we are allowed to overhear the conversation between God and Satan (vv. 6-12)—a conversation that was never revealed to Job and his friends?

4. The name *Satan* means "accuser." What is the essence of Satan's accusation against Job (vv. 8-12)?

How does his accusation lead to Job's disaster?

5. Try to put yourself in Job's place. How might you have felt as wave after wave of disaster struck (vv. 13-19)?

6. Have you ever wanted to bang on the gates of heaven, demanding an explanation for the pain you were experiencing? Why is this desire so strong within us?

7. What is astounding about Job's response (vv. 20-22)?

Why do you think he is still able to worship and praise the Lord?

8. Read Job 2. The scene in heaven repeats itself with a new twist. Why is Satan still unsatisfied with Job's character (vv. 1-5)?

9. How would Job's new affliction intensify the pain he already felt (vv. 7-8; see also 7:5, 13-14; 30:17, 30)?

10. Those who cursed God (v. 9) were to be stoned to death (see

Lev 24:10-16). How does Job respond to his wife's "solution" to his suffering?

Although Job does not answer his own question, why would it be wrong to accept good from God but not trouble (v. 10)?

11. At least in the early part of the story, what can we learn from Job's friends about supporting those whose suffering is intense (vv. 11-13)?

Bring to the Lord any pain you are currently experiencing. Ask him for strength to endure that pain without compromising your integrity.

2
Praying
Our Pain
Psalm 6

In the book *Early Widow,* Mary Jane Worden describes some of the physical and emotional pain of losing her husband:

I find that some of the very physical symptoms of those first days are diminishing: extreme shortness of breath, that choking sensation, involuntary moans, the bone-weary feeling that my whole body is made of lead, a dry mouth, heart palpitations.

There is still the stabbing, piercing pain as the realization that Jim is indeed gone sweeps over me again and again. I sometimes find myself moving about as though I am enshrouded in a thin casing of ice, like a sapling after a winter storm. *Fragile. If I move suddenly or in the wrong way, I will shatter. And then, like Humpty Dumpty, who could put me together again?"*[1]

Sometimes our pain is so great that we feel overwhelmed. During such times, we can find welcomed relief in the psalms. Eugene Peterson writes that the psalms "are provided not to teach us about God but to train us in responding to him. We don't learn the Psalms until we are praying them." Psalm 6 provides a wonderful medium for expressing our pain, anguish and doubts to God. The psalm provides very few "answers," but rather gives full vent to our questions.

1. What are some of the benefits of expressing our pain rather than internalizing it?

2. Read Psalm 6. How would you describe the mood of this psalm?

What words or phrases reveal the depth of David's suffering?

3. Why do you think David assumes that his suffering is due to God's anger or wrath (v. 1; see also Ps 38:1, 4, 18)?

4. Should we normally assume that our suffering is due to God's anger? Why or why not?

Why do people often jump to that conclusion?

5. What questions does David bring to the Lord (vv. 3, 5)?

6. In addition to "How long, O Lord," what other questions do you tend to ask during difficult times? Explain.

7. What specific requests does David make of the Lord (vv. 1-4)?

8. What do David's requests reveal about God's character?

9. What aspects of God's character do you cling to in times of anguish? Explain.

10. How does the mood of the psalm suddenly shift in verses 8-10?

11. Why do you think David is so certain that God has heard and accepted his prayer?

12. In what situations have you felt assured of the Lord's answer before it actually came?

What gave you that confidence?

13. If you are suffering or oppressed, make David's prayer your own. Quietly pray the words of the psalm. Because of God's unfailing love, trust that he has heard your prayer and will answer it.

---

[1]*Early Widow: A Journal of the First Year* (Downers Grove, Ill.: InterVarsity Press, 1989).

3
Waiting for the Lord

Psalm 27

One of Samuel Beckett's most famous plays is entitled *Waiting for Godot*. Throughout the play the characters wait and wait for Godot to appear, but he never does. The play is Beckett's way of saying that hope is futile—especially hope in God.

In contrast to Beckett's despair, the Bible offers hope to the sufferer. When we feel overwhelmed and ready to give up, Psalm 27 encourages us to "wait for the Lord." When we see no possibility of relief, David assures us, "I am still confident of this: I will see the goodness of the Lord in the land of the living."

1. In what kinds of situations do you find it hardest to wait?

2. Read Psalm 27. David's confidence in this prayer is based on God's promises to him in 2 Samuel 7:5-16 (see also v. 28). What specific items in the psalm are related to God's promises?

Why must our hope in God be based on his promises?

3. Why is David able to be fearless in the face of evil men, armies, and even war (vv. 1-3)?

4. What images of safety does David apply to the Lord in verses 1-2 and 5-6?

5. How does it give you hope to know that the Lord is your stronghold (or "mighty fortress") during battle and your shelter from life's storms?

6. David seeks not only the Lord's protection but also the Lord himself (v. 4). How is David's intense desire for God revealed in this psalm?

7. What does it mean for us to "dwell in the house of the Lord" (v. 4), "gaze upon the beauty of the Lord" (v. 4), and "seek his face" (v. 8)?

In what ways can you actively pursue these goals?

---

8. David's confident statements about the Lord (vv. 1-6) lead up to his prayer in verses 7-12. What is the substance of his prayer?

What real dangers does he seem to be facing?

---

9. The psalm ends as it begins—with David's confidence in the Lord's help (vv. 13-14). How can David's view of God help you to "be strong and take heart" in the midst of suffering?

---

10. Why must your hope not only be confident but also patient (v. 14)?

Ask God to strengthen your confidence in his promises and to make you patient as you wait for his answers.

4
The God of All Comfort

2 Corinthians 1:3-11

We have two small children, ages three and five. They are like accidents waiting to happen! At least once a day one of them will scuff his knee, fall off her bicycle, pinch a finger or stub a toe.

When they cry out in pain, we always rush to their side. Except for getting the basic facts ("What happened?"), our primary job at such times is providing comfort and support. We hold them while they cry, kiss the hurt finger, and lovingly apply a Band-Aid.

Whenever we comfort others, we imitate our heavenly Father—the God of all comfort. Second Corinthians 1 describes the comfort we receive from the Lord during our suffering and trials. It also emphasizes the important role other Christians—especially those who know God's comfort—can play during our troubles.

---

1. When you are suffering, what can others do to comfort and support you?

---

2. Read 2 Corinthians 1:3-11. How and why does God respond when we suffer (vv. 3-4)?

3. Do these verses apply only to suffering for the gospel, or do they include other types of suffering? Explain.

4. How do suffering and comfort go hand in hand (vv. 5-7)?

5. In what ways have you experienced God's comfort during times of difficulty and pain?

6. How have you been able to help others because of the suffering and comfort you have experienced?

7. In verses 8-9 Paul describes a time of intense personal pain. What words and phrases reveal the magnitude of his suffering?

8. Why is it important to learn how to rely on God rather than ourselves (v. 9) during life's trials?

How is this attitude different from passive acceptance of suffering?

9. God delivered Paul from his deadly peril (v. 10). Why is Paul so confident that God will continue to deliver him (vv. 10-11)?

10. How can God be glorified as a result of our suffering (vv. 10-11)?

11. In what situation do you need to experience God's comfort?

12. What can you do this week to extend God's comfort to someone else in pain?

Ask God to cause his comfort to flow into your life so that it can overflow to others.

5
The Power of Weakness

2 Corinthians 12:1-10

When I was three, I loved to play Superman. At first my mother pinned a towel around my neck for a cape, and I would fly around the house with my arms outstretched. Later she made me a red cape with a Superman "S" on the back.

A few years ago, I mentioned the cape to her. She disappeared into a back room and emerged with the neatly folded, tiny red costume I hadn't seen for over thirty-five years! (Mothers are like that.)

In a sense, Superman has become a myth of our culture. We feel we must be faster than a speeding bullet, more powerful than a locomotive, and able to leap over any obstacle in a single bound if we are to be successful in life.

The Bible has a very different attitude: "Not by might nor by power, but by my Spirit, says the Lord Almighty." In 2 Corinthians 12 Paul discovers that God's power is best displayed in those who are humble and weak.

1. In what ways does society reward personal beauty, power, size and strength?

How does that make you feel?

---

2. Read 2 Corinthians 12:1-10. Beginning in 11:16, Paul reluctantly began "boasting" to silence his opponents. What additional incident does he boast about in 12:1-4?

---

3. If this experience had happened to me, I would be tempted to write an entire book about it! Why do you think Paul gave such sketchy details, avoiding even his own name ("I know a man in Christ")?

Explain in your own words why Paul prefers to refrain from boasting (vv. 5-6).

---

4. Why are we often tempted to boast about our education, credentials, talents and accomplishments?

5. When Paul was tempted to float aloft with conceit, how did God nail his feet to earth (v. 7)?

What effects did Paul's "thorn" have on him?

6. Like Paul, we often assume that God's power is best displayed by *removing* our weaknesses (v. 8). Why does the Lord sometimes refuse to remove our "thorns" (v. 9)?

How would you explain in your own words the meaning of God's reply to Paul and us?

7. Scholars have speculated in vain about the precise nature of Paul's thorn. Yet, according to Paul, what various types of difficulties might qualify as thorns (vv. 9-10)?

Why has Paul learned not only to endure such thorns but to "delight" in them?

8. What weakness, insult, hardship, persecution or difficulty feels like a thorn in your flesh?

9. If God chooses not to remove your thorn, how might it be a source of his grace and power in your life?

Thank God for his sufficient grace. Ask him to perfect his power in your weakness.

6
Wounds
That Heal
Hebrews 12:1-13

At the age of seven, Glenn Cunningham and his older brother were badly burned in a schoolhouse fire. His brother died, and doctors thought Glenn would never walk again.

Refusing to accept their verdict, Glenn not only walked but began to run. He entered the 1932 and 1936 Olympic Games, winning a silver medal in the 1500-meter race. He was the fastest miler in the Amateur Athletic Union every year but one between 1933 and 1938. In 1934 he astonished the spectators by running a mile in 4:06 minutes—a world record that remained unbroken for three years.

All runners must overcome pain and hardship if they want to win. As our hearts begin to pound and our muscles start to ache, the author of Hebrews urges us not to give up but to keep on running. This chapter provides powerful incentives for completing our race.

1. Why is discipline—whether at home, at work, or in sports—essential to success?

2. Look briefly at chapter 11 of Hebrews. Who are some of the "witnesses" who surround us as we run our race?

3. Read Hebrews 12:1-13. The Greek word translated as "witnesses" (12:1) is related to the English word *martyr* and refers to those who testify. What do you suppose these witnesses are saying to us as we run?

4. The author urges us to "throw off . . . the sin that so easily entangles" (v. 1). In what ways can sin entangle us as Christians?

5. We should also "throw off everything that hinders" (v. 1). Although some things are not sinful in themselves, how might they hinder our spiritual progress? (Give examples.)

6. Just as a runner fixes his eyes on the finish line, so we are to focus on Jesus (vv. 2-4). Why is he our supreme example—and more?

7. When suffering and hardship invade our lives, why do we sometimes question God's love?

How can the "word of encouragement" (vv. 5-6) change our perception of hardship?

8. Instead of fearing hardship, why should we be more concerned about its absence from our lives (vv. 7-8)?

9. How does our heavenly Father's discipline compare with that of our earthly fathers (vv. 9-10)?

10. What are the spiritual benefits of submitting to the Father's discipline (vv. 9-11)?

11. In what sense are we like injured athletes in rehabilitation (vv. 12-13)?

12. How can cooperation with the trainer—or lack of cooperation—make a big difference in recovery for you?

Ask God for the strength to run with perseverance and the insight to see the joy that awaits you at the finish line.

7
Suffering for Christ

Acts 5:12-42

In his *Lectures to My Students,* Charles Spurgeon describes how early Methodist ministers were persecuted for preaching the gospel. One man in particular, John Furz, gives the following account:

As soon as I began to preach, a man came straight forward and presented a gun at my face, swearing that he would blow my brains out if I spoke another word. However, I continued speaking, and he continued swearing, sometimes putting the muzzle of the gun to my mouth, sometimes against my ear. While we were singing the last hymn, he got behind me, fired the gun, and burned off part of my hair.

With tongue in cheek, Spurgeon concludes by telling his students, "After this, my brethren, we ought never to speak of petty interruptions or annoyances!"

Paul warns us that "everyone who wants to live a godly life in Christ Jesus will be persecuted" (2 Tim 3:12). We may not have a gun pointed at our face or stuck in our ear, but the children of darkness will always resist the light in one form or another. In Acts 5:12-42 we learn how to respond when we suffer for Christ.

1. Briefly describe a time when you suffered because you were a Christian.

2. Read Acts 5:12-42. How would you summarize the day-to-day ac-
tivities in the temple area (vv. 12-16)?

What effects did they have on the people?

3. Why do you think the high priest and the Sadducees (those who
controlled the temple) were jealous of the apostles (v. 17)?

4. Having arrested the apostles, the high priest and his associates
called together the entire Sanhedrin—a group of seventy-one elders of
Israel—to flex their religious muscle (vv. 18-21). How and why does
the Lord mock the power of this assembly (vv. 18-26)?

5. After being given strict orders not to teach in Jesus' name, Peter and
the other apostles reply: "We must obey God rather than men!" (vv.

27-29). Give examples of when our obedience to God might conflict with our obedience to those in authority over us.

6. Why would the apostles' words make the Sanhedrin mad enough to want to kill them (vv. 29-33)?

7. What aspects of the gospel offend people in our culture?

8. How does Gamaliel, the most famous teacher of his time (and Paul's teacher before his conversion), demonstrate the wisdom for which he was famous (vv. 34-39)?

9. Each of the apostles is flogged with the traditional thirty-nine lashes and then ordered to stop speaking about Jesus (v. 40). In what ways can our obedience to God be costly today?

How has it been costly for you?

___

10. We often feel self-pity rather than joy when we suffer for Christ. What can we learn from the attitude and actions of the apostles (vv. 41-42)?

Ask God to give you a greater passion to tell others about Jesus. Pray for a greater willingness to obey him regardless of the cost.

8
The Suffering God

Mark 15:1-39

I n his book *Night,* Elie Wiesel describes how a young boy was tortured and hanged by the Nazis at Birkenbau. As the prisoners were forced to file by the dying boy, a man behind Wiesel asked, "Where is God now?" Wiesel writes: "And I heard a voice within me answer him, 'Where is He? Here He is—He is hanging here on this gallows.' "

This incident that symbolized the death of God for Wiesel became a parable of hope for Philip Yancey: "The voice within Elie Wiesel spoke truth: in a way, God did hang beside the young [boy]. God did not exempt even himself from human suffering. He too hung on a gallows, at Calvary, and that alone is what keeps me believing in a God of love."[1]

---

1. Have you ever wrestled with how a loving God could allow so much suffering and evil in the world? Explain.

---

2. Read Mark 15:1-39. Evidently, the religious leaders decided to accuse Jesus of treason rather than blasphemy (v. 1).[2] Why do you think

Jesus refuses to defend himself before Pilate (vv. 2-5)?

3. What does the incident involving Barabbas teach us about the crowd, the chief priests, and Pilate himself (vv. 6-15)?

4. The whip used for flogging (v. 15) was made of several strips of leather embedded with pieces of bone and lead. Although the Jews limited the number of lashes to thirty-nine, the Romans had no limit. How does this help you to understand Jesus' condition when he is led away into the palace (v. 16)?

5. In what additional ways do the Roman soldiers humiliate and abuse Jesus (vv. 16-20)?

Why do you think they treat him so viciously?

6. Crucifixion was usually reserved for slaves, the basest of criminals, and those who were not Roman citizens. Why would this be a horrible way to die?

7. According to Mark, how else is Jesus insulted and mocked (vv. 25-32)?

8. This is the same Jesus who earlier in Mark's account gently cleanses a leper, heals a paralytic, raises a little girl from the dead, feeds five thousand hungry people, gives sight to a blind man, and teaches people to love God and their neighbor. How then would you explain the intense hatred and hostility displayed by those present at his crucifixion?

9. The cry "My God, my God, why have you forsaken me?" comes from Psalm 22. Look briefly at that psalm, especially verses 1-21. What additional insights does it give you into Jesus' agony on the cross?

10. Why do you think Jesus' loud cry and the way he died convinced the Roman centurion that Jesus was the Son of God (vv. 33-39)?

11. How does it help you to know that God himself, in human form, has shared in our sorrows and deepest suffering?

12. How does the cross shatter the notion that God is remote, uncaring, far-removed from such horrors as the Nazi death camps or the Cambodian killing fields?

13. The author of Hebrews reminds us that we do not have a high priest who is unable to sympathize with our weaknesses (Heb 4:15). Approach Jesus now in prayer, confidently asking him for the mercy and grace you need today.

---

[1]Philip Yancey, *Where Is God When It Hurts?* (Marshall Pickering, 1991), pp. 155-56.
[2]Much of the background material related to the crucifixion is derived from *The NIV Study Bible* (Hodder & Stoughton, 1987), pp. 1527-30.

9
The Death of Death

1 Corinthians 15

I n an article entitled "Why I Like My Pie in the Sky," J. I. Packer laments over how seldom Christians today think about heaven. He writes: "When persons suffering loss of memory cannot recall where their earthly home is, we pity them; but Christians who forget that heaven is their true home, and never think positively about heaven at all, are much more to be pitied. Yet this, it seems, is how most of us proceed most of the time."[1]

Perhaps one reason we seldom think about heaven is because it seems so remote, so far-removed from our experience. We imagine ourselves as disembodied spirits, floating on celestial clouds around the throne of God.

Yet the Bible's view of eternity is much more tangible than that. Just as the dry bones in Ezekiel's vision came together at God's command and were covered with muscle and skin and filled with the breath of life, so too we will one day be raised from the dead. In 1 Corinthians 15, Paul describes this final victory—the death of death—and the comfort and encouragement it brings.

---

1. When you think of life after death, what images come to mind?

2. Read 1 Corinthians 15:1-34. According to Paul, what are the most important elements of the gospel (vv. 1-11)?

3. Why do you think Paul places such emphasis on Christ's resurrection appearances (vv. 5-8)?

4. Greek philosophy taught that the body was the prison of the soul. Any thought of a resurrection, therefore, seemed repugnant (v. 12). Yet according to Paul, what are the consequences if there is no resurrection (vv. 13-19)?

Why are these consequences so closely connected to the resurrection—especially to Christ's resurrection?

5. If there were no hope of being raised from the dead, how would it affect Paul's lifestyle—and ours (vv. 29-34)?

6. Think of non-Christians in our society. To what extent do you think their behavior and attitudes are the result of a lack of hope? Explain.

7. Because Christ has, in fact, been raised from the dead (v. 20), how does that radically change our concept of the future (vv. 21-28)?

8. Read 1 Corinthians 15:35-58. It is difficult to imagine what our resurrection bodies will be like. (How old will we be? Will we be thinner or better looking?) According to Paul, how will our resurrection bodies differ from our present bodies (vv. 35-49)?

9. Although we hate the thought of seeing our loved ones die, why would living forever in our present bodies be unthinkable and impossible (vv. 50, 53)?

How and when will we experience this change that Paul describes?

10. Although all of us will die (unless the Lord comes first), how has Christ taken away death's victory and sting (vv. 54-57)?

11. Our hope of being raised from the dead and living forever with Christ has immediate implications (v. 58). How should we live in light of this hope?

12. How can this hope encourage you in times of suffering?

Thank God for the hope of the resurrection. Pray that this hope will sustain you in times of suffering and motivate you during your earthly labors.

---

[1] *Christianity Today,* June 18, 1990.

10
The Shattered Silence

Job 38:1-41; 40:1-14; 42:1-6

Our study will end as it began—with the book of Job. After numerous chapters in which Job and his accusers wrestle with why Job is suffering, God himself finally speaks, shattering the divine silence.

Although he never gives a direct answer to Job's questions (could Job have understood it anyway?), God calls Job and us to trust him even when our suffering seems unjust and meaningless.

1. Have you ever felt that God treated you unfairly, that he owed you an explanation for why you were suffering? Explain.

2. Read Job 38. How would you describe the emotional tone of this chapter?

3. When God finally speaks, it is not with answers but questions. How would you summarize some of the questions he asks of Job?

4. What is the point of this endless barrage of questions—over seventy in chapters 38—41?

5. How do these verses show us why it is essential to remember that "as the heavens are higher than the earth, so are my ways higher than your ways and my thoughts than your thoughts" (Is 55:9)?

6. Read Job 40:1-14. What are some of the charges the Lord makes against Job?

7. When we or others we know suffer, why do you think we are tempted to question God's justice, to condemn the Lord, to justify ourselves (40:8)?

8. Why should a true vision of God's character cause us to declare with Job: "I am unworthy—how can I reply to you? I put my hand over my mouth. I spoke once, but I have no answer—twice, but I will say no more" (40:5)?

9. Read Job 42:1-6. What does Job learn about God and himself from this encounter?

10. In forty-two chapters, why do you think the Lord never directly answers Job's questions about his suffering?

11. How does it affect you to know that you may never fully understand why God has allowed you to suffer?

12. Why is trust in God even more important than understanding?

Thank God for his wisdom, power and love. Ask him for the strength to trust him even when your suffering seems unjust or meaningless.

Leader's Notes

Leading a Bible discussion can be an enjoyable and rewarding experience. But it can also be *scary*—especially if you've never done it before. If this is your feeling, you're in good company. When God asked Moses to lead the Israelites out of Egypt, he replied, "O Lord, please send someone else to do it!" (Ex 4:13).

When Solomon became king of Israel, he felt the task was far beyond his abilities. "I am only a little child and do not know how to carry out my duties. . . . Who is able to govern this great people of yours?" (1 Kings 3:7, 9).

When God called Jeremiah to be a prophet, he replied, "Ah, Sovereign LORD, . . . I do not know how to speak; I am only a child" (Jer 1:6).

The list goes on. The apostles were "unschooled, ordinary men" (Acts 4:13). Timothy was young, frail and frightened. Paul's "thorn in the flesh" made him feel weak. But God's response to all of his servants—including you—is essentially the same: "My grace is sufficient for you" (2 Cor 12:9). Relax. God helped these people in spite of their weaknesses, and he can help you in spite of your feelings of inadequacy.

There is another reason why you should feel encouraged. Leading a Bible discussion is not difficult if you follow certain guidelines. You don't need to be an expert on the Bible or a trained teacher. The suggestions listed below should enable you to effectively and enjoyably fulfill your role as leader.

Preparing to Lead

1. Ask God to help you understand and apply the passage to your own life. Unless this happens, you will not be prepared to lead others. Pray too for the various members of the group. Ask God to give you an enjoyable and profitable time together studying his Word.

2. As you begin each study, read and reread the assigned Bible passage to familiarize yourself with what the author is saying. In the case of book studies, you may want to read through the entire book prior to the first study. This will give you a helpful overview of its contents.

3. This study guide is based on the New International Version of the Bible. It will help you and the group if you use this translation as the basis for your study and discussion. Encourage others to use the NIV also, but allow them the freedom to use whatever translation they prefer.

4. Carefully work through each question in the study. Spend time in meditation and reflection as you formulate your answers.

5. Write your answers in the space provided in the study guide. This will help you to express your understanding of the passage clearly.

6. It might help you to have a Bible dictionary handy. Use it to look up any unfamiliar words, names or places. (For additional help on how to study a passage, see chapter five of *Leading Bible Discussions,* SU).

7. Once you have finished your own study of the passage, familiarize yourself with the leader's notes for the study you are leading. These are designed to help you in several ways. First, they tell you the purpose the study guide author had in mind while writing the study. Take time to think through how the study questions work together to accomplish that purpose. Second, the notes provide you with additional background information or comments on some of the questions. This information can be useful if people have difficulty understanding or answering a question. Third, the leader's notes can alert you to potential problems you may encounter during the study.

8. If you wish to remind yourself of anything mentioned in the leader's notes, make a note to yourself below that question in the study.

Leading the Study

1. Begin the study on time. Unless you are leading an evangelistic Bible study, open with prayer, asking God to help you to understand and apply the passage.

2. Be sure that everyone in your group has a study guide. Encourage them to prepare beforehand for each discussion by working through the questions in the guide.

3. At the beginning of your first time together, explain that these studies are meant to be discussions not lectures. Encourage the members of the group to participate. However, do not put pressure on those who may be hesitant to speak during the first few sessions.

4. Read the introductory paragraph at the beginning of the discussion. This will orient the group to the passage being studied.

5. Read the passage aloud if you are studying one chapter or less. You may choose to do this yourself, or someone else may read if he or she has been asked to do so prior to the study. Longer passages may occasionally be read in parts at different times during the study. Some studies may cover several chapters. In such cases reading aloud would probably take too much time, so the group members should simply read the assigned passages prior to the study.

6. As you begin to ask the questions in the guide, keep several things in mind. First, the questions are designed to be used just as they are written. If you wish, you may simply read them aloud to the group. Or you may prefer to express them in your own words. However, unnecessary rewording of the questions is not recommended.

Second, the questions are intended to guide the group toward understanding and applying the *main idea* of the passage. The author of the guide has stated his or her view of this central idea in the *purpose* of the study in the leader's notes. You should try to understand how the passage expresses this idea and how the study questions work together to lead the group in that direction.

There may be times when it is appropriate to deviate from the study guide. For example, a question may have already been answered. If so, move on to the next question. Or someone may raise an important question not covered in the guide. Take time to discuss it! The important thing is to use discretion. There may be many routes you can travel to reach the goal of the study. But the easiest route is usually the one the author has suggested.

7. Avoid answering your own questions. If necessary, repeat or rephrase them until they are clearly understood. An eager group quickly becomes passive and silent if they think the leader will do most of the talking.

8. Don't be afraid of silence. People may need time to think about the question before formulating their answers.

9. Don't be content with just one answer. Ask, "What do the rest of you think?" or "Anything else?" until several people have given answers to the question.

10. Acknowledge all contributions. Try to be affirming whenever possible. Never reject an answer. If it is clearly wrong, ask, "Which verse led you to that conclusion?" or again, "What do the rest of you think?"

11. Don't expect every answer to be addressed to you, even though this will probably happen at first. As group members become more at ease, they will begin to truly interact with each other. This is one sign of a healthy discussion.

12. Don't be afraid of controversy. It can be very stimulating. If you don't resolve an issue completely, don't be frustrated. Move on and keep it in mind for later. A subsequent study may solve the problem.

13. Stick to the passage under consideration. It should be the source for answering the questions. Discourage the group from unnecessary cross-referencing. Likewise, stick to the subject and avoid going off on tangents.

14. Periodically summarize what the *group* has said about the passage. This helps to draw together the various ideas mentioned and gives continuity to the study. But don't preach.

15. Conclude your time together with conversational prayer. Be sure to ask God's help to apply those things which you learned in the study.

16. End on time.

Many more suggestions and helps are found in *Leading Bible Discussions* (SU). Reading and studying through that would be well worth your time.

Components of Small Groups

A healthy small group should do more than study the Bible. There are four components you should consider as you structure your time together.

Nurture. Being a part of a small group should be a nurturing and edifying experience. You should grow in your knowledge and love of God and each other. If we are to properly love God, we must know and keep his commandments (Jn 14:15). That is why Bible study should be a foundational part of your small group. But you can be nurtured by other things as well. You can memorize Scripture, read and discuss a book, or occasionally listen to a tape of a good speaker.

Community. Most people have a need for close friendships. Your small group can be an excellent place to cultivate such relationships. Allow time for informal interaction before and after the study. Have a time of sharing during the meeting. Do fun things together as a group, such as a potluck supper or a picnic. Have someone bring refreshments to the meeting. Be creative!

Worship. A portion of your time together can be spent in worship and prayer. Praise God together for who he is. Thank him for what he has done and is doing in your lives and in the world. Pray for each other's needs. Ask God to help you to apply what you have learned. Sing hymns together.

Mission. Many small groups decide to work together in some form of outreach. This can be a practical way of applying what you have learned. You can host a series of evangelistic discussions for your friends or neighbors. You can visit people at a home for the elderly. Help a widow with cleaning or repair jobs around her home. Such projects can have a transforming influence on your group.

For a detailed discussion of the nature and function of small groups, read *Small Group Leaders' Handbook* or *Good Things Come in Small Groups* (both from IVP).

Study 1. When Your World Falls Apart. Job 1—2.
Purpose: To identify with Job's grief and painful sense of loss.

Question 1. Every study begins with an "approach" question, which is meant to be asked before the passage is read. These questions are important for several reasons.

First, they help the group to warm up to each other. No matter how well a group may know each other, there is always a stiffness that needs to be overcome before people will begin to talk openly. A good question will break the ice.

Second, approach questions get people thinking along the lines of the topic of the study. Most people will have lots of different things going on in their minds (dinner, an important meeting coming up, how to get the car fixed) that will have nothing to do with the study. A creative question will get their attention and draw them into the discussion.

Third, approach questions can reveal where our thoughts or feelings need to be transformed by Scripture. That is why it is especially important not to read the passage before the approach question is asked. The passage will tend to color the honest reactions people would otherwise give because they are, of course, supposed to think the way the Bible does. Giving honest responses before they find out what the Bible says may help them see where their thoughts or attitudes need to be changed.

Questions 2-3. Throughout history, people have wrestled with the problem of evil, especially with the question of why the innocent suffer. Logic would seem to dictate three possible solutions to the problem: (1) God is not all-powerful and therefore cannot prevent suffering, (2) God is not completely just and good and therefore allows the innocent to suffer, or (3) those who suffer are not innocent and therefore deserve their fate.

Unlike the Greeks or the Western philosophers, the Israelites never questioned God's power or goodness; these were foundational to their theology. Therefore, when someone suffered, the conclusion was self-evident—the person had done something to deserve the suffering.

Although this conclusion seemed inescapable in the abstract, it did not always fit the facts, as we see in the story of Job. In order to solve this enigma, the reader is allowed to overhear a conversation in heaven between the Lord and Satan. During that conversation, the Lord affirms that Job is "blameless and upright, a man who fears God and shuns evil."

Armed with this knowledge from the beginning of the story, the reader is forced to conclude that suffering sometimes defies the neat logic of the three possibilities discussed previously.

Question 4. Satan claims that Job's righteousness is merely evil in disguise. Job serves God only because it pays to do so, not because of any true moral or spiritual qualities. (The same accusation could be made against *any* person who seems to love and serve God.) Satan claims that if God were to remove his blessings from Job's life, his true evil nature would be revealed. God takes up the challenge in order to prove the genuine nature of Job's love and loyalty.

Questions 8-9. Although Job had lost his family and possessions, he was still physically healthy—a great blessing from God. Satan claims that this blessing must also be removed in order to expose the self-serving nature of Job's righteousness.

The precise nature of Job's sickness is uncertain, but its symptoms were painful festering sores over the whole body (7:5), nightmares (7:14), scabs that peeled and became black (30:28, 30), disfigurement and revolting appearance (2:12; 19:19), bad breath (19:17), excessive thinness (17:7; 19:20), fever (30:30) and pain day and night (30:17)." *(The NIV Study Bible* [Hodder & Stoughton, 1987], p. 736)

Question 11. Christians are often quick to lecture those who suffer. Although such words are often well intended and biblical, they ignore the legitimate pain or sense of loss the person feels. Sometimes silence is better than a sermon and our mere presence is more supportive than a lecture.

Study 2. Praying Our Pain. Psalm 6.

Purpose: To encourage people to imitate the psalmist—or even to make his words their own—by honestly expressing their anguish, pain and doubts to God.

Question 2. In early Christian liturgy, Psalm 6 was considered one of the seven penitential psalms (the others were Psalms 32, 38, 51, 102, 130 and 143). The occasion of the psalm was evidently a time of severe illness for David, possibly brought on by sin (see v. 1). The mood is one of agony (v. 2), anguish (v. 3) and sorrow (v. 7).

Question 3. The first verse of Psalm 38 begins with exactly the same words as Psalm 6. In Psalm 38, David confesses that he is guilty (v. 4) and admits that he is troubled by his iniquity and sin (v. 18). In neither psalm, however, are we told the specific nature of David's sin, nor are we told the occasion.

Question 4. After people have a chance to answer, you might want to briefly review the conclusions of the previous study. The book of Job emphasizes that our suffering is not necessarily related to sin.

Question 7. Notice the verbs in verses 1-4: "Do not rebuke me . . . or discipline me," "be merciful," "heal me," "turn . . . and deliver me," "save me."

Question 8. Although David believes that his suffering is due to God's anger and wrath, he maintains his high view of God's character. David realizes that God is merciful (v. 2), a healing physician (v. 2), a savior (v. 4), and a God of infinite and unfailing love (v. 4).

Question 9. When suffering and anguish invade our lives, many people begin to doubt God's love, mercy and care. Like the Greek and Western philosophers (see leader's note to study 1, question 2), they conclude that God could not be loving and allow them to experience such pain.

Like David, we need to cling to our faith in God's character during the bad times as well as the good. When we fail to do so, we fulfill Satan's accusation against Job—we serve God only because he rewards us and as long as he keeps our lives tranquil and free from pain.

Question 10. Because David is so confident of God's mercy and unfailing love, he can also be confident that the Lord has heard and will answer his prayer. If our prayers lack confidence, we may have too low a view of God.

David's confidence is also based on God's promises to Israel (see Deut 7:9, 12) as well as to David and his dynasty (see Ps 89:24, 28, 33; 2 Sam 7:15; Is 55:3). In order to have the degree of confidence David exhibits, we must base our requests on what God has promised.

Study 3. Waiting for the Lord. Psalm 27.
Purpose: To encourage those who are suffering to "wait for the Lord."

Question 2. David's assurance that he has nothing to fear from his enemies (vv. 1-3) is based on God's promise in 2 Samuel 7:11. His confidence that he will see the goodness of the Lord in the land of the living (v. 13) is based on the promises in 2 Samuel 7:9-16. God had promised that David's name would be great, Israel would be established in the land, David would have rest from his enemies, he would have an offspring, and his kingdom would be established forever. These promises gave David great confidence in times of stress and affliction.

Our faith, too, must be grounded in God's promises. Sometimes we are told that if our faith is strong enough or if we "name it and claim it" God will definitely answer our prayers. Yet such assumptions can be naive. John tells us, "This is the confidence we have in approaching God: that if we ask anything according to his will, he hears us. And if we know that he hears us—whatever we ask—we know that we have what we asked of him" (1 Jn 5:14-15). Only those prayers that are according to God's will are answered. And the best way to know God's will is to look at what he has commanded and promised.

Question 4. The word "light" (v. 1) often symbolized well-being and life (see Ps 97:11). A "stronghold" was a fortress that protected people from their enemies. David knew, therefore, that God was the source of his life and well-being, his Savior from all potential harm, and his protection from his enemies.

David also refers to the Lord as the one who keeps him safe, who hides and shelters him, and who will exalt him (vv. 5-6).

Question 6. David's primary prayer in this psalm is not for protection but rather for the privilege of dwelling in the house of the Lord all the days of his life (v. 4). He desires nothing more than to seek the Lord (vv. 4, 8) and to gaze on his beauty (v. 4). David also wants to learn from the Lord and be guided by him so that he can walk in "a straight path" (v. 11). These are the requests of a man who is passionately devoted to his God.

Question 8. "Hear my voice . . . be merciful to me" (v. 7); "Do not hide your face from me, do not turn your servant away in anger" (v. 9); "Do not reject me or forsake me" (v. 9); "Do not turn me over to the desire of my foes" (v. 12). These are the prayers of a man who seeks deliverance from real and present dangers.

What are those dangers? The psalm mentions enemies in verses 2 and 6. An attacking army and war are mentioned in verse 3. Foes and false witnesses are described in verse 12.

Question 10. Hebrews 11:1 tells us that "faith is being sure of what we hope for and certain of what we do not see." By faith, David was confident that his prayers would be answered, but he also knew that he needed to wait patiently for those answers. Genuine faith does not expect or demand instant results.

Study 4. The God of All Comfort. 2 Corinthians 1:3-11.

Purpose: To consider how we can comfort others during their suffering, just as the Father comforts us.

Question 2. God responds by comforting (or consoling and encouraging) us in all our troubles. Notice that he does this for two reasons. First, he comforts us because he is compassionate (v. 3). The Lord truly cares for us and therefore desires to comfort us when we are afflicted. Second, he comforts us so that we can comfort others, following his example and drawing on our own experiences of being comforted by God. In such cases we become instruments of God's comfort to others.

Question 3. In this context, Paul's primary thought is suffering for Christ and for the sake of the gospel (vv. 5-7, 8-11). Yet our Father is "the God of *all* comfort" (v. 3, my emphasis). Likewise, because he is "the Father of compassion" (v. 3), he cares for "all our troubles," not just those related to the gospel.

Question 7. Notice the words and phrases: "hardships," "suffered," "great pressure," "far beyond our ability to endure," "sentence of death," "raises the dead," "deadly peril" and "deliver." Paul could scarcely pile more words on top of each other in such a brief space. His suffering was extreme!

Question 8. A key principle throughout 2 Corinthians is that God displays his power to us and others through our weaknesses. Our suffering brings God's comfort (1:3-11); our "jars of clay" reveal the "treasure" of the gospel (4:7-12); even though we may be timid and unimpressive (10:1-18), we fight with divine weapons that can demolish strongholds; and God's grace is sufficient for us in every type of suffering or hardship (12:1-10).

God usually glorifies himself in the midst of our weaknesses rather than by removing them (although that, too, can glorify God), because our weaknesses highlight his power, not our own. Those who are personally powerful are often tempted to glorify themselves.

Study 5. The Power of Weakness. 2 Corinthians 12:1-10.

Purpose: To discover that God's grace is sufficient for every situation. To realize that God's power is best displayed in those who are humble and weak, not in those who are strong and proud.

Question 2. Paul was caught up into the "third heaven" (v. 2), which is synonymous with "paradise" (v. 3). (The first heaven is the earth's atmosphere; the second heaven is the realm of the stars and planets.) Paul is not sure whether his remarkable experience took place in his body or out of the body—and he doesn't seem to care (vv. 2-3). Although such experiences would be marvelous to describe, Paul was not permitted to tell them to others (v. 4).

Question 3. As mentioned previously, Paul was not permitted to describe the details of his vision (v. 4). Yet the sketchy nature of verses 1-4 go beyond God's prohibition. Paul tells us in verse 6 that he refrains from boasting "so that no one will think more of me than is warranted by what I do or say."

In other words, Paul wanted people to evaluate him on the basis of his everyday words and actions rather than by a list of impressive credentials (a principle we certainly could use today!). Also, Paul realizes that God gave him "a thorn in [his] flesh" to keep him from boasting and becoming conceited (v. 7).

Some have suggested that Paul is describing some other person rather than himself ("I will boast about a man like that," v. 5). Yet in verse 1 Paul claims that he will go on boasting, describing visions and revelations of the Lord. But he would have nothing further to boast about if the experience he recalls happened to someone else. In verse 7 Paul mentions that he was given a thorn in his flesh "to keep me from becoming conceited because of these surpassingly great revelations." That statement would make no sense unless the "great revelations" were Paul's own.

Question 5. Paul's experiences were so incredible, so extraordinary that he struggled with pride. As an apostle, he knew he was a member of Christ's most elite corps. And his spiritual experiences were so spectacular that even the other apostles, not to mention "ordinary Christians," were tempted to envy him. But before he had a chance to become conceited, to soar aloft with feelings of superiority, God nailed his feet to earth: "To keep me from becoming conceited because of these surpassingly great revelations, there was given me a thorn in my flesh, a messenger of Satan, to torment me" (v. 7).

For centuries people have speculated about the precise nature of Paul's thorn. They have suggested it was headaches, earaches, eye disease or malarial fever. Others have claimed it was epilepsy, a speech impediment, hypochondria, deafness or remorse for persecuting Christians. Still others have suggested gallstones, gout, rheumatism, a dental infection—even lice!

Whatever it was, Paul didn't like it. "Three times I pleaded with the Lord to take it away from me" (v. 8). The thorn not only kept Paul humble, it tormented him and made him feel weak. So he prayed and prayed for its removal.

Question 6. God's answer surprised Paul: "But he said to me, 'My grace is sufficient for you, for my power is made perfect in weakness' " (v. 9). Instead of removing Paul's thorn, God gave him the grace to endure it. Instead of taking away Paul's weakness, God used it to demonstrate his power.

The same principle applies to us. Notice that the Lord did not say, "My power is make perfect in your *thorn,*" but rather, "My power is made perfect in *weakness*" (v. 9). In other words, it doesn't matter whether we can identify the precise nature of Paul's thorn. God's promise applies to anything that makes us feel weak, humble and dependent on God.

Questions 7-8. Paul mentions weaknesses, insults, hardships, persecutions and difficulties (v. 10). None of the items in Paul's list is exactly the same as his thorn. But because they shared certain points of similarity with the consequences of his thorn, Paul knew God's grace was sufficient for them all.

The same is true today. We probably don't suffer from the same kind of thorn Paul did. But we too face weaknesses, insults, hardships, persecutions and difficulties—things that humble us and make us dependent on God. Whatever the nature of our thorn, like Paul we can confidently rely on Christ's grace and power.

Study 6. Wounds That Heal. Hebrews 12:1-13.

Purpose: To understand how God uses suffering and discipline to make us more like him.

Question 2. The author imagines an athletic contest in a large amphitheater. The "witnesses" include the heroes of faith mentioned in chapter 11: Abel, Enoch, Noah, Abraham, Sarah, Isaac, Jacob, Joseph, Moses' parents, Moses, the Israelites, Rahab and others. They are both the spectators in the stands who watch us run and the inspiring examples who have completed the race before us.

Questions 4-5. Runners in ancient times would strip off all their clothes before a race to allow themselves maximum freedom of movement. The author compares sin to loose-fitting clothes that could become entangled in our legs and trip us. Yet sin is not the only thing that can keep us from running our best race. Many areas of life are neutral in themselves but can hinder us from running if we become too absorbed in them or if they distract us from our primary goal. Encourage the group to think of specific examples.

Question 6. Jesus is our ultimate example because he endured extreme suffering during his race and yet kept going because of the joy that awaited him at the finish line (v. 2). Whatever we may have to suffer as Christians, it cannot compare to the crucifixion.

Yet Jesus is far more than our example. He is the author of our faith (v. 2) because he took the initiative to bring us to himself. He is also the perfecter of our faith (v. 2) because he will ultimately bring us to full maturity at the end of the race. He is with us throughout the race.

Questions 7-8. During times of suffering and hardship, many people question God's love. They wonder how a loving Father could allow them to experience such pain.

The author of Hebrews takes the opposite view. Hardship and suffering are a sign of God's love, just as discipline is a sign that a father loves his children.

The Lord is not sadistic; he does not discipline us in order to make us feel pain but rather to make us share in his holiness (v. 10).

The author also challenges the assumption that freedom from pain and hardship is a sign of God's blessing. On the contrary, if our lives are usually free from suffering we may not be members of God's family.

Questions 11-12. Because of the effects of sin in our lives, we are like injured athletes in rehabilitation (vv. 12-13). Our arms are feeble, our knees are weak, and we are lame. If we submit to the trainer's exercise program, we will become stronger and experience God's healing. But if we resist God's discipline and training, we will become permanently disabled (v. 13).

As people respond to these questions, encourage them to answer both from the text and from personal experience.

Study 7. Suffering for Christ. Acts 5:12-42.

Purpose: To consider how we should respond when we suffer for Christ.

Question 3. In order to understand the jealousy of the high priest and the Sadducees, it is helpful to understand something of their background. "The Sadducees were rather boorish, being rude to their peers as to aliens, and counting it a virtue to dispute with their teachers. They had no following among the populace, but were restricted to the well-to-do. They were more severe in judgment than other Jews. Many, but not all, priests were Sadducees; nearly all Sadducees, however, appear to have been priests, especially of the most powerful priestly families. . . .

"The Sadducees are marked for their conservatism. They denied the permanent validity of any but the written laws of the Pentateuch [the first five books of the Old Testament]. They rejected the later doctrines of the soul and its after-life, the resurrection, rewards and retributions, angels and demons" *(New Bible Dictionary,* p. 1055).

By preaching that Jesus had been raised from the dead, the apostles were challenging the Sadducees' teaching that there was no resurrection. By repeatedly declaring that some of the Jews and their leaders had been responsible for Jesus' death (see 2:23; 3:13-15; 4:10-11), the apostles were implying the guilt of the religious leaders (v. 28). And because the apostles had a large following among the people, they were threatening the status of the high priest and the Sadducees as the primary religious authorities.

Question 4. The Sanhedrin was "the supreme Jewish court, consisting of 70 to 100 men (71 being the proper number). They sat in a semicircle, backed by three rows of disciples of the 'learned men,' with the clerks of the court standing in front" *(The NIV Study Bible,* p. 1652). The Lord mocks the power of this assembly by demonstrating that they were ultimately powerless over the apostles, whom he could release at will.

Question 5. Urge the group to consider a variety of relationships: employer/ employee, government/civilian, officer/soldier, and so on.

To make the discussion more interesting, you might want to mention a specific situation. For example, how should we respond if our company asks us to suppress damaging product information that is important for the safety of consumers? Do we simply refuse to obey and risk losing our job, or are there other legitimate actions we might take?

Question 7. One of the most offensive aspects of the gospel in our culture is its exclusiveness. Many people would be glad to grant that Jesus is a savior or one way to God among many. But when we claim that he is the *only* way to God, it makes people furious. Our culture will tolerate almost anything but intolerance.

Many people in our society are also offended by the concept of sin. They would prefer to say that a person suffers from low self-esteem, is the victim of others' behavior, or is even insane, rather than admit that the person might actually be sinful and guilty before God.

Question 9. In this passage the apostles choose to obey God rather than men, and their decision results in a painful flogging. Yet our obedience can be costly even when we face no external challenge to God's authority. For example, in the book *L'Abri,* Edith Schaeffer mentions that during the late sixties, when she and her husband were inviting young non-Christians into their home, there was great personal cost. Their best dishes were broken, people vomited on their rugs, men and women with venereal disease slept between their sheets, and the Schaeffers sacrificed their personal privacy. It is easy to think in extremes when discussing suffering for Christ, saying, for example, that we would be willing to die for Jesus. But in what practical, everyday ways are we willing to pay the price of obedience? Encourage your group to think in these terms.

Study 8. The Suffering God. Mark 15:1-39.

Purpose: To realize that God did not exempt himself from human suffering. Because he hung on the cross at Calvary, the Lord knows the depths of our pain and anguish.

Question 2. Pilate was the Roman governor of Judea from A.D. 26 to 36. Although his official residence was in Caesarea, when he came to Jerusalem he stayed in a palace built by Herod the Great. The trial of Jesus took place at this palace, which Mark refers to as "the Praetorium" (v. 16).

The Sanhedrin decided to take Jesus to Pilate because only the Romans had the authority to execute criminals. Yet they realized that their charge of blasphemy would be meaningless to Pilate and would not be a capital offense. Therefore, they decided to accuse Jesus of treason, a crime against Rome itself and one that was punishable by death.

History tells us that Pilate was already on shaky ground with Caesar. If Pilate refused to convict Jesus of treason, the religious leaders could charge him with disloyalty to Rome.

Why didn't Jesus defend himself before Pilate? The same question could be asked of Jesus' silence before the Sanhedrin in chapter 14. Perhaps his silence was due to the fact that both trials were a mockery of justice. Although Jesus had done nothing illegal, the chief priests and the Sanhedrin were looking for excuses to put him to death before his trial even began (14:55). They also brought in false witnesses to try to incriminate him (14:56). Ultimately, Jesus was condemned by the Sanhedrin for telling the truth (14:62-65).

Jesus also knew of the political pressure Pilate was under. Such pressure made Pilate's own self-preservation far more important to him than giving a fair trial to an unknown Jew. In such circumstances, a defense would be useless. Yet because Jesus refused to offer a defense, Pilate was forced by Roman law to pronounce against him.

Question 4. Victims of Roman flogging often did not survive. Jesus' severe condition is evident from the fact that he was too weak to carry his own cross (15:21).

Question 6. "Crucifixion was practiced by the Phoenicians and Carthaginians land later used extensively by the Romans. Only slaves, provincials and the lowest types of criminals were crucified, but rarely Roman citizens. . . . The condemned man was stripped naked, laid on the ground with the cross-beam under his shoulders, and his arms or his hands tied or nailed (Jn. 20:25) to it. This cross-bar was then lifted and secured to the upright post, so that the victim's feet, which were then tied or nailed, were just clear of the ground, not high up as so often depicted. The main weight of the body was usually borne by a projecting peg, astride which the victim sat. There the condemned man was left to die of hunger and exhaustion. Death was sometimes hastened by breaking of the legs, as in the case of the two thieves, but not done in our Lord's case, because he was already dead" *(New Bible Dictionary: Second Edition* [InterVarsity Press, 1982], p. 253).

Question 9. Because Psalm 22 so aptly fitted the circumstances of Jesus' crucifixion, he quoted from it while on the cross. The psalm depicts a righteous sufferer who feels forsaken by God because of the insults, taunts and attacks of his enemies. Yet the psalm concludes with a strong declaration of faith in God's deliverance (vv. 19-31).

Study 9. The Death of Death. 1 Corinthians 15.

Purpose: To renew our hope in Christ's final victory—the death of death—and to realize the comfort and encouragement it brings.

Question 2. Christ's death, burial and resurrection are the key elements of the gospel. He died "for our sins" (v. 3), taking on himself the punishment we deserved. "He was buried" (v. 4)—a proof that he was really dead. He was also raised from the dead by God the Father, "the firstfruits [or first of many] of those who have fallen asleep" (v. 20).

Question 3. Paul lists six resurrection appearances here (to Peter, the twelve, more than five hundred people, James, and Paul himself), although the Gospels mention more. By claiming that most of the five hundred people who saw the resurrected Jesus were still alive, Paul was saying in essence: "If you don't believe me, ask them!" Both the testimony of Scripture and the testimony of eyewitnesses confirm Paul's assertion that Jesus rose from the dead. If his resurrection is accepted, then there can be no ultimate objection to the idea of a general resurrection.

Question 4. "Some at Corinth were saying that there was no resurrection of the body, and Paul draws a number of conclusions from this false contention. If the dead do not rise from the grave, the (1) 'not even Christ has been raised' (v. 13); (2) 'our preaching is useless' (v. 14); (3) 'so is your faith' (v. 14); (4) we are 'false witnesses' that God raised Christ from the dead (v. 15); (5) 'your faith is futile' (v. 17); (6) 'you are still in your sins' (v. 17) and still carry the guilt and condemnation of sin; (7) 'those also who have fallen asleep [have died] in Christ are lost' (v. 18); and (8) 'we are to be pitied' who 'only for this life . . . hope in Christ' (v. 19) and put up with persecution and hardship" *(The NIV Study Bible,* p. 1756).

Question 5. If human destiny, as Ernest Nagel claims, is "an episode between two oblivions," then it is utterly foolish to risk the only life we have in preaching a gospel that cannot preserve us beyond the grave. We might as well spend our brief time in hedonistic pleasure. A recent Nike commercial says the same thing: "Life is short; play hard."

Question 7. Christ's resurrection assures us that those in Christ will experience life beyond the grave. Paul hints at what that life will be like in verses 21-28. At Christ's coming, he will resurrect those who belong to him (v. 23). His reign will culminate in the destruction of all forces, powers and authorities that oppose him, including death itself (vv. 24-26). Then Christ will hand the kingdom over to the Father (vv. 24, 27-28).

Questions 8-9. Our present bodies are perishable (v. 42), not just in the sense that they die, but also because they can be cut, broken, bruised and disabled in countless ways. Our resurrection bodies—both in whole and in part—will not be subject to that kind of wear and abuse. They will be both imperishable and immortal (see also v. 53).

Our present bodies are sown in dishonor (v. 43). For example, anyone who has seen someone waste away with cancer can testify of the pain and humiliation that such people experience. Yet however dishonorable the physical circumstances of our death, Paul assures us that our resurrection will be glorious, full of the honor due to those in Christ.

Our present bodies are also weak (v. 43). We tire easily, get sick, and require constant care and attention to keep us healthy. In contrast, our resurrection bodies will be powerful in both health and vigor.

Finally, our present bodies are natural (v. 44). Notice that Paul does not contrast natural with physical but rather with spiritual. Our resurrection bodies will be physical, but they will not come from the dust of the earth (v. 47); instead, they will have a heavenly origin (v. 48).

Christ's own resurrection gives us many clues about what our future bodies will be like. You might want to read the various resurrection accounts in the Gospels as preparation for this study.

Question 10. In John 11:25-26, Jesus proclaims, "I am the resurrection and the life. He who believes in me will live, even though he dies; and whoever lives and believes in me will never die." Several years ago I caught a glimpse of the power of this promise when I was asked to speak at a funeral. A good friend's father had passed away, and his family needed encouragement and hope. Under the circumstances, that hope could only come by understanding the two aspects of Christ's claim.

First, I explained that Jesus is "the resurrection." Although death seemed to be victorious over the woman's father, the victory was temporary. The day would come when her father would be raised from the dead, never to die again. As Jesus put it: "He who believes in me will live, even though he dies."

But Christ's promise also gives us immediate, not just future, hope. He goes on to say that "whoever lives and believes in me will never die." Although the man's body had died, *he* had not died. He was (and is) more fully alive now than he had ever been during his earthly existence.

Both aspects of Christ's promise—the immediate hope of being alive with him after death and the future hope of being raised from the dead—remove the victory and sting of death. They can provide great comfort when we lose someone we love or when we face our own death.

Study 10. The Shattered Silence. Job 38:1-41; 40:1-14; 42:1-6.

Purpose: To realize that God calls us to trust him even when our suffering seems unjust and meaningless.

Question 2. Notice that the Lord answers Job out of a storm (v. 1). The storm could symbolize several things: anger at Job for questioning God's actions, the power and might of God, or the awesome majesty described in 37:22. The barrage of questions also seems to come in the form of a challenge.

Questions 3-4. The Lord never intends for Job to answer his questions—they are rhetorical, and Job must plead ignorance to each one. The questions humble Job and put him in his place. In effect, the Lord says to Job: "If you cannot understand the mysteries of the universe, how could you possibly understand the reasons for your suffering, even if I explained them to you?"

The questions also call Job (and us) to trust in God's wisdom and goodness. If he is wise and good enough to run the universe, then surely we can trust him with our lives.

Questions 6-7. In 19:6, Job had said, "God has wronged me." The Lord challenges that accusation by asking: "Would you discredit my justice? Would you condemn me to justify yourself?" (v. 8).

Whenever we sit in judgment on God, assuming that our standards are higher than his and our decisions are wiser than his, we say in effect that we are better than God. The Lord challenges Job and us to prove our boast of divinity by speaking in thunderous tones, adorning ourselves with glory and splendor, humbling the proud and crushing the wicked (vv. 9-13). If we can do all that, then the Lord says he will admit that we (as gods) can save ourselves (v. 14). Yet if we cannot do these things, then the Lord expects us to let him be God and to stop questioning his decisions.

Questions 10-12. In chapter 23 Job states the intense desire he has felt throughout the book: "If only I knew where to find him; if only I could go to his dwelling! I would state my case before him and fill my mouth with arguments. I would find out what he would answer me, and consider what he would say" (vv. 3-5). But when the Lord finally does appear in chapters 38-42, Job asks no questions, and the Lord gives no direct answers!

Yet if God had to explain himself and seek our approval every time he did something we could not understand, what kind of relationship would that be? Certainly it would not be one of faith and trust. Rather, we would be trusting in our own judgment and wisdom to decide what is best—for ourselves and the rest of the universe. Of course, God does not and will not play by these rules.

Instead of seeking our approval, the Lord enlarges our vision of his wisdom, might, power, justice and love. He demonstrates that he is worthy of our trust, even when we cannot understand why he does what he does. At the same time, the book of Job humbles us, pointing out what should be painfully obvious: We are unworthy to question the Lord's character or his decisions.

Jack Kuhatschek is the editor of Lamplighter Books at Zondervan Publishing House. He is the author of several books, including Taking the Guesswork out of Applying the Bible, *the LifeBuilder Bible Studies* Romans, Galatians, David, Self-Esteem, Leading Bible Discussions *and the booklet* How to Study the Bible. *Jack, his wife, Sandy, and their two children live in Grand Rapids, Michigan.*